"Sexual harassment is not
only bad for victims,
it is also bad for business."

– ACADEMY OF MANAGEMENT

STOP
Workplace
Sexual Harassment,
Quickly & Permanently

Printed in the United States of America
13-digit ISBN: 978-1-885228-52-9

Credits

Copy Editor	Kathleen Green, Positively Proofed, Plano, TX info@PositivelyProofed.com
Design, art direction & production	Melissa Farr, Back Porch Creative, Frisco, TX info@BackPorchCreative.com

CONTENTS

"I allowed a workplace culture to take root in my office that was too permissive and decidedly unprofessional. It accommodated destructive gossip, offhand comments, and off-color jokes... and that was wrong."

– U.S. REP. BLAKE FARENTHOLD, resignation letter

INTRODUCTION

Can your workplace pass this test?

First, consider every possible professional relationship: superiors, peers, customers, clients, vendors, students, professors, mentors, recruiters, coaches, and human resource professionals.

Next, imagine every industry, location, and situation in which work is conducted: office, off-site, factories, hospitals, meetings, conventions, classrooms, planes, hotels, restaurants, bars, office parties, phone, email, text, social media and handwritten notes.

Now, without any prior explanation or discussion, ask every person with whom you professionally interact to define **sexual harassment**.

Did *everyone's* answer include these three conditions?

1. The unwanted behavior is severe and/or pervasive enough to cause a hostile work environment

2. The behavior is perceived as offensive (regardless of the offender's intent)

3. A reasonable person must find the behavior offensive

The slightest variance in answers equals the gap in which violations can occur, with devastating consequences.

Why everyone should care

Workplace sexual harassment hurts everyone, men and women, at every level of the organization. Even if you've never personally experienced it, you cannot escape its cumulative effects: a demoralizing, fearful, and deceitful culture. Sound like an environment you'd like to work in? Probably not.

To be clear, sexual harassment is a violation of U.S. civil rights law and, therefore, illegal. That should be reason enough to stop it. If you need more reasons, just know that the way employees are treated is tied directly to the bottom line, and sexual harassment is just plain bad for business.

When did giving a compliment become a crime?

By themselves, words and gestures mean nothing. People provide the meaning and context. That's why some may claim the term "sexual harassment" is too subjective to enforce. What one person passes off as flattery or a joke, someone else might perceive as offensive. How can you know?

Making it clear

Once you understand the mindset and behaviors of sexual harassment, there's no mistaking it. That's why this handbook is filled with multiple examples of specific behaviors and situations to eliminate any confusion. And once you know, you can't not know. In other words, claiming ignorance is not an excuse for bad behavior. Education and accountability go hand in hand. Here's what you're about to learn:

- Myths and facts about sexual harassment

- Legal definition of sexual harassment

- Specific behavioral and situational examples

- Common ways sexual harassment is excused

- Why sexual harassment is not always about sex

- What targets and bystanders can do and perpetrators must do

- Conditions of a positive, respectful work culture

Major transgressions are often the result of accumulated minor ones. If you overlook the red flags, you'll be left asking, how did this happen? Instead, this handbook aims to help you become an organization that can confidently state: *This is why nothing happened.*

"I would call my female assistant 'hot pants' or 'sex pants' when I was yelling to her from the other side of the office. Something I thought was funny at the time, but then realized I had completely demeaned and belittled her to a place of non-existence."

– MORGAN SPURLOCK, filmmaker/TV producer

The goal of this handbook is bold – to stop workplace sexual harassment quickly and permanently. In order for that to happen, certain things can no longer be tolerated:

ST⬤P Ignoring signs of disrespect

ST⬤P Excusing, defending, or minimizing demeaning behavior

ST⬤P Blaming victims

ST⬤P Making it difficult to report an alleged offense

ST⬤P Retaliating against anyone who resists or speaks up

ST⬤P Neglecting the negative business impact of sexual harassment

ST⬤P Assuming that a one-time training will provide adequate education and understanding of the topic

You'll also learn several things to start doing that will help your organization establish and maintain a positive workplace culture. By starting the conversation at what constitutes a respectful, professional, and productive work environment, it becomes even more clear why there's no place or justification for sexual harassment.

Training is a process, not an event

We invest time and money in things we value. So, how much does your organization value a safe and respectful culture? The answer is evident in how much time and serious education is dedicated to sexual harassment awareness and prevention training for every employee.

In the last year, what percentage of training in your organization do you believe was dedicated to these topics?

Product awareness _____%

Technical skills _____%

Interpersonal skills ___%

Customer service _____%

Safety _____%

Professional development _____%

Personal development ____%

Leadership development ____%

Sexual harassment awareness _____%

No matter the results, your training in sexual harassment prevention starts today with this handbook! Whether you're reading independently or your organization provided you with this handbook, you now have an excellent resource for ongoing education.

Be proactive

To be effective, sexual harassment training cannot be a one-time event. This is *not* about covering your bases to prevent a lawsuit. (If that's the current thinking, it only reveals the necessity and urgency of the message.) This is about establishing respect and dignity for all employees as the norm, not the exception. Permanently stopping workplace sexual harassment requires consistent education.

The ultimate goal is to bring everyone together equally rather than segregate. After all, that would only be another form of discrimination. This handbook provides the core information you'll need to lay the foundation.

Make training even more relevant by supplementing this with industry-specific examples and situations. Chapter 7 provides a place for employees to add their own ongoing insights about sexual harassment and behaviors to STOP. Here are more ways to make your training successful.

Making the message stick

- ✔ **Treat it seriously.** Any suggestion that this information is a joke undermines its purpose.

- ✔ **Focus on behaviors.** Show versus tell. What do you say or do to convey respect or disrespect?

- ✔ **Include bystander intervention.** Teach bystanders how to support victims instead of remaining silent and complicit.

- ✔ **Create a safe learning environment.** Establish ground rules upfront for respectful communication.

- ✔ **Encourage discussion.** Information changes nothing; action does. Facilitate discussions and ways to apply ideas.

- ✔ **Use industry-specific examples.** Ask participants to provide potential "sticky situations" and share appropriate responses to clear up any misunderstandings.

- ✔ **Follow up.** Support employees in how to share concerns, file reports, and seek healthcare options to treat distress related to workplace incidents.

"Sexual harassment is unwelcome sexual behavior which can offend, humiliate, or intimidate others.
It can be physical, verbal, or written. Sexual harassment is not professional, logical, or productive."

– LINDA SWINDLING, JD

WHAT IS
SEXUAL
HARASSMENT?

Definition of Sexual Harassment

"Sexual harassment is unwelcome sexual advances, requests for sexual favors, and other verbal or physical conduct of a sexual nature."
– Equal Employment Opportunity Commission

This is the first sentence in the EEOC's legal definition of sexual harassment. It may be short, but it's loaded with content. Before moving forward with other concepts, let's unpack a few key terms. First, sexual harassment happens in the *workplace* – so what is that exactly?

"Workplace"
The workplace includes any setting in which work is conducted, which may be unique to your industry. This includes a physical office, fieldwork or institution, but also every other location where work-related business takes place, such as:

- Social events
- Professional conferences
- Business travel
- Training events
- Business meals
- All communication by phone, email, text, social media or handwritten

Basically, if the reason for your location or relationship is because of your job duties, then it counts as "workplace." A workplace therefore extends to locations and working hours outside of the standard eight-hour workday. Sexual harassment can happen any day of the week, at any time.

Based on the explanation of "workplace," here are examples of inappropriate behaviors.

1. *A sales manager and associate drive together to call on a customer. During the ride, the sales manager plays music containing sexually explicit lyrics that the associate finds offensive.*

2. *After work, several employees attend Friday night happy hour. A supervisor sits next to an employee, buys him a drink, and puts her hand on his leg.*

3. *After being rejected once, an employee sends multiple late-night text messages to a co-worker asking for date.*

"Unwelcome sexual advances"

Based on how much time we spend at work, it's not uncommon to meet, date, and develop serious relationships with people with whom you share common interests. However, this type of relationship is very different from sexual harassment, which is predatory and includes unwelcome sexual advances. These advances are not the result of **mutual** attraction, but rather a way of establishing control through an imbalance of power.

Sexual advances are unwanted if one or more of the following is true:

- A person believes that submission to the conduct is necessary in order to get or keep a job.

- A person believes that employment decisions such as shifts, assignments, raises, promotions, and demotions depend on whether he or she submits to or rejects the conduct.

- The conduct interferes with a person's work performance or creates an intimidating, hostile, or offensive working environment.

Unwelcome does not mean "involuntary." A victim may consent or agree to certain conduct and actively participate in it even though it is offensive and objectionable. That's because sexual harassment is based on abuse of power and a culture that allows it. Victims fear the repercussions of rejecting unwanted advances.

A major indicator of unwanted sexual advances is that they are one-sided. *Victims do their best to avoid uncomfortable situations, not initiate them.* The mindset of both victims and perpetrators is more thoroughly explained in Chapter 3. For now, understand that sexual conduct is unwelcome whenever the person subjected to it considers it unwelcome.

Based on the explanation of "unwanted sexual advances," here are examples of inappropriate behaviors:

1. *While riding the elevator alone together, an employee suddenly turns to a co-worker and forcibly kisses the individual.*

2. *Every time a male delivery driver walks into an office with a package, a group of females refer to him as "sexy" and gather to watch him walk out. The driver feels embarrassed.*

3. *A single mom living paycheck to paycheck requires a certain shift so that she can get her child on the school bus. A supervisor promises to help her out only if she'll have sex with him, so she does.*

"Other verbal or physical conduct of a sexual nature"

The behaviors of sexual harassment can be overt and covert, meaning that some are extremely obvious and others are merely suggestive. Any communication, verbal or nonverbal, that is of a sexual nature can be considered sexual harassment when it is severe or pervasive enough to negatively impact the work environment. Here are specific examples:

Verbal or written

- Making inappropriate sexual comments about clothing, appearance, personal behavior or a person's body

- Telling sexual or sex-based jokes

- Sending unwanted suggestive letters, notes, texts, or emails

- Requesting sexual favors, making sexual innuendos, or repeatedly asking someone out who is not interested
- Sharing sexual anecdotes or stories of your personal sex life
- Inquiring about someone's sexual activities or history
- Telling lies or spreading rumors about someone's sex life
- Name calling, mocking, insulting
- Making derogatory remarks about a person's sexual orientation or gender identity
- Using sexualized nicknames or pet names in place of a person's given name

Physical
- Blocking a person's physical movement or path
- Inappropriate and unwanted touching of a person, including kissing, hugging, patting, pinching, stroking, rubbing, or massaging
- Touching oneself in a sexually suggestive manner
- Inappropriate and unwanted touching of someone's clothes, uniform, hair, jewelry, or nametag
- Standing uncomfortably close
- Following too closely or stalking
- Purposefully brushing up against another person

Nonverbal
- Giving unwanted personal gifts
- Playing music with lewd, sexually suggestive lyrics

- Looking a person's body up and down

- Whistling, howling, or staring in a sexually suggestive or offensive manner

- Making facial expressions, such as winking, throwing kisses, or licking lips

- Making obscene or offensive gestures

Visual

- Displaying posters, drawings, pictures, magazines, or screensavers that are sexual in nature (even in a "private" locker or on a personal phone or computer)

- Sharing sexually inappropriate images or videos, such as pornography, with co-workers, even on work breaks and even if the co-workers viewing it are not personally offended. What matters is how this behavior negatively impacts the entire work environment

Based on the explanation of "other verbal or physical conduct of a sexual nature," here are examples of inappropriate behaviors.

1. *Two employees consistently discuss their dating life in detail, including sexual escapades, loudly enough so that others can hear.*

2. *An employee has a sexually suggestive screen saver on the computer.*

3. *A boss comes up behind an employee and says, "It looks like you've had a hard day," then gives an uninvited shoulder massage.*

Do the right thing

So, you can see that a one-sentence legal definition of sexual harassment covers a lot. But, here's the thing – you don't need a legal definition to know if what you're doing is right or wrong.

"The test would be if you go to work, have experiences, and go home and tell your family about it and be proud of what went on."

— JIM HACKETT, CEO, Ford Motor Company

A simple litmus test for knowing the difference between professional behavior and sexual harassment is asking these questions:

- *Would I behave this way if I knew my colleagues were watching?*

- *Would I behave this way if I knew my family was watching?*

- *Would I behave this way if I knew my actions would be reported in the news?*

- *Would I do or say this to every single person I work with, regardless of job title or gender?*

- *How would I feel if a member of my family was treated this way?*

- *Would I feel comfortable with our most important customer, board member, or the public viewing my professional work environment?*

Doing the right thing needs no explanation. Your intentions and actions are aligned – there are very few, if any, misunderstandings. If you're feeling the stress of covering up information, lying, or worrying other people would "get the wrong idea," that's a major hint that behaviors need changing.

If the majority of people recognize that sexual harassment is wrong, why does it happen?

"It's not about what men don't know. It's about what men have known too well: that we can get away with it. That it will be excused, hidden, justified and rationalized, and no one will be called to account."

— SHAWN VESTAL, columnist,
Spokesman-Review (Spokane, WA)

Sexual harassment cannot exist unless the environment supports it. Awareness of behaviors is one thing, but unless there are consequences for bad behavior, nothing changes. Just like a virus doesn't attack only one part of the body, sexual harassment is not episodic. It's systemic. Let's continue with a few more definitions. Ask yourself: Have I ever witnessed or experienced this behavior in my workplace?

Types of sexual harassment

As you now know, sexual harassment comes in many forms. However, there are two primary types of sexual harassment. Let's take a look at the definitions.

1. **Quid Pro Quo.** The Latin term *quid pro quo* translates to "one thing in return for another." In this case, an employee's benefits, such as hiring, firing, promotion, demotion, job assignments, or pay raises are based on the acceptance or rejection of unwelcome sexual advances.

This applies to employment situations and any other situation in which the harasser has a superior position to the victim.

"It was a quid pro quo: 'I have power, you want access, sleep with me – or I'm going to be really mean to you the next day. And there will be consequences.'"
— DREW DIXON, former executive, Arista Records

Examples of quid pro quo:

1. *A student is struggling in her college chemistry class. Her professor invites her to his office for additional help where he makes sexual advances, assuring her he intends to give her a good grade.*

2. *A doctor promises to include a nurse on an elite surgical team if the nurse will agree to meet for drinks.*

3. *A customer threatens to give a huge sale to another company if the sales rep rejects unwanted sexual advances.*

4. *An employee offers sexual favors in return for a pay raise.*

2. **Hostile Work Environment.** This term refers to situations in which an employee is exposed to offensive sexual materials or comments and/or unwelcome sexual contact or advances. To be sexual harassment, it must be considered severe or pervasive. It does not have to be both.

The law generally doesn't prohibit simple teasing, isolated offhand comments, or incidents that happen only once and are not serious. So, generally speaking, a single unwanted request for a date or one sexually suggestive comment that offends you and/or was inappropriate may not be "severe" or "pervasive." However, a single incident of very serious conduct, like unwanted physical contact, would probably meet this part of the definition of sexual harassment.

Harassment that is less severe but happens frequently or persists over time may be "pervasive," and therefore also meets this part of the definition. So, a number of relatively minor separate incidents may add up to sexual harassment if the incidents negatively affect your work environment. A hostile work environment may be created by co-workers, a supervisor or employer, or even customers or clients.

 Examples of a hostile work environment:

1. *A female bookkeeper works in an auto repair shop. The male mechanics tend to use coarse language and use humor filled with sexual innuendos. In addition, the restroom shared by the employees is adorned with posters of nude women, which the female employee finds offensive. She mentioned these issues to the shop owner who told her, "They're just joking around."*

2. *During weekly group brainstorming meetings, the boss regularly communicates that an idea is "boring" by simulating masturbation. Everyone knows that means you should "shut up" and let someone else with a better idea talk. Several employees begin calling in sick rather than attend these meetings.*

3. *A big vendor insists on working with a particular company rep. The vendor calls frequently to discuss business but ends up asking about the rep's personal life and sharing intimate details. The rep asks to get off the account but is told that dealing with "quirky" personalities is part of the job.*

Let's get real

Have you ever contributed to a hostile work environment by behaving in a way that made someone else uncomfortable?

Have you ever been uncomfortable at work due to a hostile work environment?

Are you aware of any examples of this taking place in your organization?

If you answered "yes" to any of these questions, then more questions are needed. What allows this behavior to continue? What changes need to be made right now to end a culture of harassment and create one of respect?

Other terms you should know

In addition to understanding what sexual harassment is, there are a few other terms you should know. All of them involve unacceptable behavior that negatively impacts the workplace environment.

Sexism. An attitude of a person that he or she is superior to a person of the opposite sex. For example, a man thinks that women are too emotional. Or a woman thinks that all men are chauvinists.

Sex discrimination. Behaviors that occur when employment decisions are based on an employee's sex or when an employee is treated differently because of his or her sex.

For example, in a coed workplace, a female supervisor always asks the male employees to move the boxes of computer paper. Or, in a coed workplace, a male supervisor always asks the female employees to plan office parties.

Sexual misconduct. State laws vary on defining acts that constitute sexual misconduct. It's safe to say that all the behaviors described as sexual harassment also count as sexual misconduct. Organizations may have a specific policy that is more expansive or more limited than state laws.

The term can apply to consensual and non-consensual acts, because if the two people involved work together, a sexual relationship of any kind might be forbidden by their employer; or if one person is of higher stature in the organization, that power can be used as coercion or might lead to professional retribution.

Sexual assault. According to the U.S. Department of Justice, this is "any type of sexual contact or behavior that occurs without the explicit consent of the recipient." Examples include forced sexual intercourse, attempted rape, child molestation, incest, fondling, and forcible sodomy.

The major distinction between sexual harassment and sexual assault is sexual harassment's connection to the victim's employment and/or work performance, which is why sexual harassment is a civil rights issue.

Sexual assault is a crime against another person. However, unlike sexual harassment, it has nothing to do with the person's employment and/or work performance, it is a criminal assault, of a sexual nature, against another person.

Moving past definitions

OK, we've covered the basic definitions and provided examples of sexual harassment. You may have learned some new things, or been tempted to skim over material that you've already been taught in past trainings. Maybe it all seems like common sense.

Whatever the case, it's time to get serious about creating a workplace culture where men and women are treated equally and with respect. Remember, awareness does not create change. **Action does!**

"Was I aware that other high-level male employees were having sexual relationships with female staffers? Yes. Did these female staffers have access to information and wield power disproportionate to their job titles? Yes. Did that create a hostile work environment? Yes. Did I believe these female staffers were benefiting professionally from their personal relationships? Yes. Did that make me feel demeaned? Completely. Did I say anything at the time? Sadly, no."

> – NELL SCOVELL, former staffer,
> *Late Night with David Letterman*

10 Reasons Why Sexual Harassment Is Bad for Business

1. Sexual harassment contradicts the organization's stated values and principles.

2. Sexual harassment tarnishes an organization's public reputation.

3. Sexual harassment creates negative customer perceptions.

4. Sexual harassment breeds a hostile work environment, causing high turnover.

5. Sexual harassment makes it difficult to recruit, hire, and retain top talent.

6. Sexual harassment causes increased stress and conflict in the workplace.

7. Sexual harassment lowers creativity and productivity.

8. Sexual harassment decreases employee trust and engagement.

9. Sexual harassment increases absences and sick leave.

10. Sexual harassment leads to an increased risk of lawsuits based on inappropriate behavior.

"It doesn't matter who makes the offense. It could be a manager, co-worker, or even a non-employee like a client, contractor, or vendor. If the person's conduct creates a hostile work environment or interrupts an employee's success, it is considered unlawful sexual harassment."

– ALYSON DOYLE

2.

RECOGNIZING SEXUAL HARASSMENT

Who, What, When, and Where

How often does sexual harassment occur? What industries are most affected? Are the victims always female?

You can know the definition of sexual harassment and still not be able to identify it based on your assumptions. Your assumptions are ideas you take for granted as being true, even without proof. What you assume to be true or right is influenced by many factors, such as your age, gender, culture, education, and personal experiences.

If you're like most people, you've probably misinterpreted a situation once or twice because of faulty assumptions. It's always better to act on the facts. Let's test some of your assumptions about sexual harassment and see if they're correct based on facts provided by the Equal Employment Opportunity Commission (EEOC).

True or false?

Read these statements and decide if they're true or false. Afterward, we'll take a look at each one so you can compare your assumptions with the facts.

___ Fewer than 30% of women have experienced some form of sexual harassment.

___ You can be a victim of sexual harassment even if you're not directly harassed.

___ Sexual harassment victims are always women.

___ Sexual harassment is limited to interactions between male bosses and female subordinates.

___ Sexual harassment is most prevalent in the entertainment industry.

___ A person cannot legally consent to sex if he or she is intoxicated.

___ Sexual harassment ends when the recipient firmly rejects unwanted sexual advances.

Separating myths from facts

Remember, any inaccurate assumptions you may hold about sexual harassment will affect the level at which you recognize and address it. Let's see how you did.

Fewer than 30% of women have experienced some form of workplace sexual harassment.

False. Surveys indicate that a whopping 88% of women report having experienced sexual harassment. Research suggests women of color, in particular, often must confront the combined impact of racial, ethnic, and gender prejudice.

"The only women who don't believe that sexual harassment is a real problem in this country are women who have never been in the workplace."
    – CYNTHIA HEIMEL, author

You can be a victim of sexual harassment even if you're not directly harassed.

True. Anyone who is affected by the offensive conduct,

whether the intended target or not, is a victim of sexual harassment. For example, an observer could experience a hostile work environment without being the direct recipient of inappropriate behavior.

Or, if one employee is granted a promotion in return for sexual favors, other male and female co-workers can allege sexual harassment by showing that they were denied an equal opportunity for promotion because of the improper sexual conduct.

Sexual harassment victims are always women.
False. Both perpetrators and victims can be of either gender, and the perpetrator is not necessarily someone of the opposite gender. Surveys indicate 79% of victims are women; 21% are men.

Sexual harassment is limited to interactions between male bosses and female subordinates.
False. You know from the previous answer that sexual harassment isn't limited by gender. It's also not limited to certain relationships. Sexual harassment can occur between peers, people who previously dated, boss to subordinate and vice-versa, customers, vendors, suppliers, professors, and students.

Sexual harassment is most prevalent in the entertainment industry.
False. Hollywood stories make flashy headlines, and it can appear that sexual harassment is a problem only in the most elite circles. The reality is, it's taking place every day in work settings just like yours.

> *"A lot of these things are power issues, they're not sex issues."*
>
> — AMY BRANDWEIN, chef

A person cannot legally consent to sex if he or she is intoxicated.

True. Sexual consent is an agreement to participate in a sexual activity. People who are drunk, high, or passed out can't consent to sex. There are also laws to protect minors, under the age of 18, from being pressured into sex with someone much older than them.

Here are a few more basics regarding consent:

- **Freely given.** Consenting is a choice you make without pressure, manipulation, or under the influence of drugs or alcohol.

- **Desired.** When it comes to sex, you should only do stuff you want to do, not things that you believe you're expected to do.

- **Specific.** Saying "yes" to one thing (like kissing) doesn't mean you've said "yes" to others (like having sex).

- **Current circumstances.** Just because you agreed to something in the past doesn't imply you're OK with it now. Consent is required every time.

- **Informed.** You can only consent to something if you have all the details about the person and situation.

- **Reversible.** You can change your mind about what you feel like doing, any time.

Sexual harassment automatically stops when the recipient firmly rejects unwanted sexual advances.

False. Many times the harasser retaliates by creating a hostile work environment or, if in a position of authority, threatens termination. That's why permanently stopping sexual harassment requires the support of the entire organization, versus putting the burden on the victim alone to stop it.

So, how'd you do? If you responded to all seven statements correctly, congratulations! You're on track to being part of the solution. For any statements where you disagreed, consider the facts. It can be jarring to have your assumptions challenged, but it's nowhere near the trauma of experiencing sexual harassment.

He Said, She Said, or We Said

Here are three scenarios describing potentially inappropriate workplace behaviors. Put yourself in the shoes of the target (regardless of your gender) and imagine that you personally had to hear, witness, and experience the same things. Would you call it sexual harassment?

1. You are a member of an elite college band in which upperclassmen assign rookies highly sexualized nicknames. Rookie band members may be called on to perform "tricks" based on their nickname.

2. You are a female U.S. trial attorney. During an office happy hour, your supervisor gropes your breasts and buttocks and makes sexually charged comments. In the same office, another senior male attorney hacks

a female colleague's personal email account and conducts a cat-fishing operation by creating a fictitious online profile to entice her.

3. You work in a manufacturing plant where a male supervisor tells a female subordinate, "I want to screw you so bad." Another employee describes in pornographic detail what he wanted to do to another woman before exposing himself. Those who complain face retaliation from co-workers and bosses.

Crossing the line

These scenarios aren't fiction – they really happened. Each was determined by a court of law to be sexual harassment. In all cases, the accused initially denied the allegations.

The first scenario includes examples detailed in an investigative report of The Ohio State University's Marching Band. Director Jonathan Waters was fired for allowing what the university called "a sexualized culture conducive to sexual harassment."

The second example took place within the U.S. Justice Department. In his investigative report, Inspector General Michael Horowitz stated that the supervising attorney accused of groping was transferred but received no suspension or loss in pay or grade.

Finally, the third scenario includes incidents reported at two Ford assembly plants in Chicago. The EEOC reached a $10 million settlement with Ford for sexual and racial harassment.

> *"I came of age in the '60s and '70s, when all the rules about behavior and workplaces were different. That was the culture then. I have since learned it's not an excuse, in the office — or out of it. To anyone."*
>
> – HARVEY WEINSTEIN,
>   fired Hollywood producer (apology letter)

When sexual harassment is part of the cultural norm, how do you know if it's truly inappropriate? If it's merely a case of he said/she said – which person is telling the truth? How do you protect yourself against false accusations?

These are all valid questions and, luckily, the law has already addressed them. The way to move past he said/she said is to widen the scope of opinions.

Reasonable person standard

If you're trying to assess if some conduct that has taken place is actually harassing conduct, the way to determine it is to use the "reasonable person" standard. If a reasonable person in the same or similar circumstances would find the conduct intimidating, hostile, or abusive, then it's probably harassment.

The reasonable person standard includes consideration of the perspective of persons of the same race, color, religion, gender, national origin, age, or disability as the harassment victim (*not* the offender). For example, if a female employee complains of harassment, make sure in applying this test that you take the perspective of a woman, not a man. If, in the perspective of another woman, you would find this conduct as harassment, it probably is.

Although harassing conduct must be **objectively** viewed as creating a hostile work environment to be unlawful, the subjective perception of the particular harassed employee is still significant. If the employee does not perceive the work environment to be hostile because of that conduct, the conduct is not unlawful harassment.

For example, if five co-workers, four male and one female, are telling "blonde jokes," and none of the employees finds them offensive, hostile, or abusive, the conduct is not harassment. However, it's also not very professional and could be viewed as harassment depending on who's in the room.

Three perspectives

Another way to think of the reasonable person standard is to filter any action you take through three perspectives:

- Your viewpoint

- Recipient's viewpoint

- Outside observer's viewpoint

The outside observer offers an unbiased viewpoint, without benefit of explanation or insider information – just based on appearances. If all three sets of eyes interpret the situation as fair, reasonable, ethical, safe, and respectful – it probably passed the reasonable person standard.

> "*If your flirting strategy is indistinguishable from harassment, it's not everyone else that's the problem.*"
> – JOHN SCALZI, author

That's (not) just the way it is

Minimizing or justifying bad behavior is the breeding ground for a hostile work environment. Here are 10 common excuses used to brush sexual harassment under the carpet and pretend it's no big deal. If you've heard or used any of these phrases, there's already a problem.

ST⬡P

Accepting These 10 Excuses for Sexual Harassment

1. **"You should be flattered."** Telling another person how to feel is controlling and, therefore, demeaning. If you really want to give a sincere compliment, praise the person's professional skills and abilities.

2. **"Everybody knows that's just the way it is – deal with it."** Just because everyone recognizes that an individual behaves inappropriately doesn't make it OK. In fact, it makes it worse. If everyone knows, everyone needs to speak up. Otherwise, you're part of the problem.

3. **"It was a joke."** If the target doesn't think it's funny, it's not funny.

4. **"I didn't mean anything by it."** What you intended doesn't matter. What counts is how your actions are received. If what you say or do is perceived as hostile or pressured sexual advances, it's wrong.

5. **"Boys will be boys."** It's insulting to men to suggest they can't control themselves, as if they have no choice. Plenty of men choose to behave in a respectful

manner. Every individual must be held accountable for personal choices, regardless of gender.

6. **"I was drunk."** You are 100% responsible for what you say or do, even if intoxicated. Also, if you're getting drunk on the job, there are more problems going on here.

7. **"Look at the way she's dressed. She's asking for it."** Nobody asks to be the recipient of unwanted sexual advances, and the victim is never to blame for someone else's choices. Even if a woman is attractively dressed, she gets to choose whom she desires. Do not assume it's you. If anyone's attire is inappropriate according to workplace dress codes, the proper response is to reiterate requirements, not make advances.

8. **"It's all in your head."** This could be true. But, if inside the person's head your behavior makes him or her uncomfortable, then it does. Remember the reasonable person standard? If another person similar to the target shares the same perception, then the behavior is inappropriate.

9. **"But, he's such a nice guy."** A person can be nice, committed, charismatic, and even a supporter of women's rights – and still engage in sexual harassment. Positive public personas don't cancel out sexual misconduct behind closed doors.

10. **"It only happened once."** One time is too many, especially if it was considered severe. It means the offender felt safe enough in the current work culture to behave inappropriately. Sexual harassment isn't an isolated event; it's systemic. If it happened once, it's likely to happen again.

"Every woman of my vintage
knows what sexual harassment is,
although we didn't have
a name for it."

– RUTH BADER GINSBURG,
    U.S. Supreme Court Justice

3.

PSYCHOLOGY OF SEXUAL HARASSMENT

Profile of a Perpetrator

Can you tell who is likely to sexually harass? It turns out you can, thanks to years of research conducted by prominent psychologists. It is most often men with specific personality traits in combination with opportunity.

According to psychologist John Pryor, Ph.D., when individuals with a proclivity for sexual harassment are placed in social situations that permit or accept this sort of behavior, the behavior is most likely to occur. That's why the only way to permanently stop sexual harassment is to change the social norms of the entire organization.

What's gender got to do with it?

Perpetrators can be either gender and the same or opposite sex as the victim. But, research indicates that overwhelmingly it's men who commit sexual harassment against women. Part of the reason has to do with biology; the other with who's in power.

Louise Fitzgerald, a psychologist at the University of Illinois at Urbana-Champaign says that science supports what most of us know: There are behavioral differences between the sexes.

> *"It's not like women are somehow immune from dark personality traits. But we know from gender research that men are more aggressive, more socialized to seek sex and believe they have a right to it."*

That last part, "believe they have a right to it," has to do with power. Statistically, there are more men than women in leadership positions, (which makes the case for promoting more women as one way to eliminate sexual harassment).

"Power creates this perfect mental storm for misconduct."

— JONATHAN KUNSTMAN,
assistant professor of psychology,
Miami University at Ohio

Remember, you don't have to be a high-level executive to have power. It all depends on the social hierarchy of your particular organization and situation.

Likelihood to Sexually Harass = Power + Environment

Psychologist John Pryor invented a test to measure a man's tendency to harass. The "Likelihood to Sexually Harass" scale is a test consisting of 10 scenarios. Here's an example:

> *Imagine that you are an executive hiring a new administrative assistant. A female candidate explains she desperately needs the job and looks at you in a way that possibly conveys she is attracted to you. How likely are you to:*
>
> - *Give her the job?*
> - *Offer the job in exchange for sexual favors?*
> - *Ask her to go to dinner to discuss the job?*

Over the years, Pryor and others have used socially engineered situations in laboratories to study how well the test predicts people's behavior. And over time, they've identified these factors as the most distinctive in harassers:

- Lack of empathy

- Belief in traditional gender sex roles

- Tendency toward dominance/authoritarianism

They also found in studies that the environment surrounding such harassers has a huge effect. If you put men who score high on the scale in situations where the system allows them freedom from punishment, they will take advantage.

Four warning signs

In a similar vein, Dr. Ellen Hendriksen, psychologist, identified four traits common among perpetrators of sexual harassment. The first two are fairly self-explanatory; the last two dive deeper into the psyche.

1. **Working in a male-dominated field.** Sexual harassment is well-documented to be more prevalent in traditionally masculine fields, like military, police, surgery, finance, science, technology, engineering, and math.

2. **Hostile attitudes toward women.** A deep hatred or disdain for women built on the belief that they are inferior.

3. **Dark triad personality.** This describes a constellation of three personality traits: Machiavellianism, psychopathy, and narcissism. A person possessing even one of these traits can make your life miserable. In combination – you've got someone who is a master of exploitation with zero remorse.

Machiavellianism describes amoral, deceitful behavior used to ruthlessly gain power. Psychopathy means to be insensitive, lacking empathy, and conscience. (A person with this trait can appear charming but quickly become volatile). Finally, narcissism is the seeking of admiration and an expectation of special treatment.

4. **Moral disengagement.** Based on the work of social psychologist Albert Bandura, moral disengagement describes the process by which an individual convinces himself that ethical standards do not apply to him within a particular situation or context. It can be further broken down into four categories:

- *Reconstructing immoral conduct.* The person tells himself a story or context that makes the behavior seem acceptable.

  Sounds like: Fired journalist Charlie Rose, in his public letter of apology after eight women accused him of sexual harassment said, "I always felt that I was pursuing shared feelings, even though I now realize I was mistaken."

- *Diffusing responsibility.* The person blames others, the situation, or the context as the reason for his actions.

  Sounds like: Actor Kevin Spacey blaming alcohol when he responded to Anthony Rapp's allegation that Spacey propositioned him when he was 14 with, "If I did behave as he describes, then I owe him the sincerest apology for what would have been deeply inappropriate drunken behavior."

- **_Dehumanizing the victim._** It's easier to hurt others by reducing them to labels, objects, or nameless faces.

  Sounds like: Following new-hire orientation training at Ford's Chicago assembly plant, female employees reported being paraded on the assembly plant floor as male workers called out, "Fresh meat!"

- **_Misrepresenting injurious consequences._** Speaking in euphemisms to minimize unflattering behavior, such as telling a "little white lie."

  Sounds like: In his court deposition for sexual assault charges, comedian Bill Cosby referred to sexual encounters as "rendezvous" and explained that drugging young women with Quaaludes was, "the same as a person would, say, have a drink."

The personality of a perpetrator can appear to be a bundle of contradictions. The person can be both charming and sinister; a champion of equal rights and patronizing; a protective confidant and opportunist. Once the dark side comes out, though, the motive and signs become very clear.

That was awkward, but was it sexual harassment?

The question that often comes up when talking about sexual harassment is how to categorize its severity. Is it a matter of degrees? Is every person who throws out a bad pickup line committing a crime or is there room for clumsy misunderstandings?

Let's draw a distinction between unwanted sexual _advances_ – (perpetrator) and unwanted sexual _attention_ (bad pickup line person), because both involve feeling uncomfortable. Yet, there's a big difference between pressured coercion and an awkward moment. One involves fear and intimidation with the threat of repercussions; the other is based on misread social cues. It's potentially rude but harmless.

Psychotherapist Marty Klein suggests that managing unwanted attention, sexual or not, is part of life: "Stories from strangers on airplanes, awkward compliments from co-workers, grocery clerks sympathetically inquiring about the brace on your wrist or that cold medicine you're buying."

These social exchanges may be momentarily awkward, but they're not a crime. They can be rebuffed by simply saying, "No, thanks," or "You read me the wrong way," and walking away. Then, it's over. No harm, no foul. When it comes to sexual harassment, though, there is harm, and the term "victim" is not used lightly.

Impact on Victims

Victims of sexual harassment are negatively impacted, often in ways you can't see. The responses vary in degree, length, and complexity, but make no mistake about it – just because you can't see the damage doesn't mean it's not there.

The extent of the emotional impact depends on a lot of factors like age, self-esteem, availability of resources, support, past incidents, gravity of offense, and history. Past trauma has a cumulative effect.

Previous to the current incident, a person may have experienced bullying, abuse, discrimination, or any other number of hardships. Behavior that you may consider to be minor may trigger a severe emotional response, even post-traumatic stress.

Here are some common responses a victim of sexual harassment might experience, emotional and otherwise.

Common emotional effects of sexual harassment

- Difficulty trusting others

- Anger and blame

- Shock

- Numbness

- Loss of control

- Disorientation

- Helplessness

- Sense of vulnerability

- Fear

- Self-blame/guilt for "allowing" the crime to happen

Common mental effects of sexual harassment

- Post-traumatic stress disorder (PTSD), including flashbacks, nightmares, severe anxiety, and uncontrollable thoughts

- Depression, including prolonged sadness, feelings of hopelessness, unexplained crying, weight loss or gain, loss of energy or interest in activities previously enjoyed

- Suicidal thoughts or attempts. (If you or someone you know is feeling suicidal, contact the National Suicide Prevention Lifeline at 1-800-273-8255.)

- Lowered self-esteem

- Self-harm such as cutting

- Self-medicating with drugs and/or alcohol

- Dissociation, including not feeling present in everyday situations
- Lack of concentration, forgetfulness
- Heightened sense of alertness, startling easily
- Racing thoughts, inability to sleep

Collateral damage

The negative effects of sexual harassment reach beyond emotions. Physical health and emotional health are closely linked, with internal symptoms manifesting externally. A victim may experience changes in appetite leading to weight fluctuations, headaches, and sleep disturbances. Stress can cause an increased risk of high blood pressure and a weakened immune system. Lack of trust and depression can lead to social isolation.

There are financial consequences as well. Poor mental and physical health can spiral into absenteeism, sick leave, and rising healthcare costs. Broader career repercussions include termination, loss of job references and networking, and promotions. Victims may choose to leave a current position to avoid a hostile environment, cutting their career advancement short.

Victims of sexual harassment lose $4.4 million in wages and 973,000 hours in unpaid leave each year in the United States.

— EQUAL RIGHTS ADVOCATES' LAW CENTER

Why some victims stay silent

You may be wondering, if experiencing sexual harassment is so bad, why don't victims just say something? To fully understand why a victim says nothing, or has a delayed response, you must first imagine what it's like to feel powerless.

"I didn't publicly share my experiences as well as many other things because for years we were conditioned to stay silent and honestly some things were extremely painful."
– GABBY DOUGLAS, Olympic gold medal gymnast

Go back to your school days – why does the small kid who is being picked on by a bully twice his size not run straight to the teacher? Why not have your parents come in and fight the battle? The answer is clear: fear of retaliation. Perpetrators don't target equals; there's always a power deferential. Here are some reasons why victims stay silent:

- Fear of retaliation (based on threats and actual evidence)
- Fear of not being believed
- Fear of further embarrassment, humiliation
- Fear of victim-blaming, feeling "weak" or guilty
- Fear of job loss and necessary income
- Fear of being labeled "promiscuous" or "a problem"
- Fear of blacklisting
- Fear of breaking a non-disclosure agreement

One-sided fear is a necessary ingredient of sexual harassment –
that is, the victim fears repercussions, but the perpetrator has no
fear of consequences. The goal, though, is not to gain compliance
through fear. Who wants to show up to work every day only to
walk on eggshells? The goal is to merely level the playing field.
In the following chapters, you'll find strategies to create a
culture of mutual respect.

"Don't be ashamed of your story...
it will inspire others."

- AMY REES ANDERSON

HOW TO RESPOND
TO WORKPLACE
SEXUAL
HARASSMENT

What to Do if You're a Victim

As you've learned so far, sexual harassment can vary in severity and pervasiveness; therefore, choosing an appropriate response will depend on the situation – and the person. The point is, you have options. You don't have to stay silent and you don't have to remain a victim.

If you don't feel comfortable addressing the incident on your own or it's too severe, seek internal help immediately. Remember, if you're reading this at work, you and your organization have the same goal: to stop sexual harassment quickly and permanently internally. You are encouraged to address inappropriate behavior as soon as possible and expect support from your organization.

3 Steps to Address Sexual Harassment
Step 1: Document
Sexual harassment in the workplace can be one unexpected event or a series of inappropriate incidents. An accurate and detailed written log, or diary, of the incident(s) will help prove your claim of sexual harassment by providing evidence of what took place and when.

When to record an incident
It's best to record an incident as soon as you believe you have experienced sexual harassment. Even if you have no intention of bringing a claim, or even if you aren't sure whether something constitutes harassment, it is important to record it.

Sexual harassment cases often start with one or two isolated remarks or incidents. You will want to be able to show the timeline and evolution of the harassment. It is also important that you write down what happened while your recollection is still fresh and accurate.

What to document

It's better to write too much rather than not enough. You may not be able to tell now whether something will be important. You should record:

- Offensive conversations or remarks

- Sexual contact or touching

- Sexual incidents in the workplace

- Emails, memos, and texts you have received (place hard-copies in your log, if possible)

- Complaints you have made: when, to whom, what you said, and the response

- Evidence of retaliation, such as being fired, lost promotions, demotions, poor performance evaluations, reassignments to a less desirable position, shift, or location, or any other concrete negative employment action taken against you because you rejected a sexual advance or other conduct based on your sex

Your incident description or log should include the names and titles of the people involved, as well as the dates and times of the incidents or conversations. If there were any witnesses, record their names. Describe how the incident affected you and your work. *Do not save this information on a work computer.* Instead, keep all notes at home in a safe place.

Also, save any harassing emails, documents, or other physical evidence of the harassment. For example, if a sexual harassment incident involves unwanted gifts, keep these items, along with detailed information about when and where the harasser gave them to you.

Document all possible evidence of your performance, such as memos and performance evaluations. In some cases, the accused party may try to claim that your charge is due to your work performance.

Step 2: Communicate

What to say in the moment

Your ability to speak up in the moment depends on the severity of the incident and the emotional impact it causes. Remember, you have options, so choose the most appropriate response for the circumstances.

Let's start with a minor incident and one that you feel confident addressing immediately. Make your message brief and clear:

- *"Stop! What you're doing is inappropriate."*

- *"Your actions are making me uncomfortable. Stop right now."*

- *"This is not professional behavior. It needs to stop immediately."*

- *"What you said just crossed the line. Don't say it again."*

- *"This isn't a joke. Stop it."*

- *"Remember that sexual harassment handbook we received? This is a behavior you need to stop."*

Speak firmly and assertively, using direct eye contact. Make it clear that this is not a "suggestion" or an option. This specific behavior must STOP. Document your conversation.

Schedule a formal meeting
If the original incident caught you off guard and you felt unprepared to speak, you can also schedule a formal meeting. This can be done privately, or with a third party present to act as a witness. (Again, document the meeting and conversation.)

Since this will be after the fact, be very specific when speaking. Include these details:

- When and where the incident occurred

- Specific behavior that was offensive

- Impact of behavior on you and your work performance

- Request for the behavior to stop immediately

It's helpful to write these details down and provide a copy to the other person so you can both date and sign.

Can I record conversations?
Before you choose this form of proof, know the laws of your state. Otherwise, you could be the one doing something illegal. Most states have a one-party consent rule. That means as long as you're a participant in the conversation, you can record at will. But, in all-party consent states, everyone involved must give permission for the conversation to be recorded. The laws can get tricky, so if in doubt, it's best not to record.

Put it in writing
Communicating in writing provides a paper trail of proof and can be an emotionally safer choice in some circumstances. You

can also communicate in person and follow up with written documentation. Keep copies of all correspondence at home, not at work. There are several forms this can take:

- Registered letter with proof of receipt

- Email

- Text

Detail the behaviors that are offensive in the communication, including dates, times, locations, and any witnesses. Note if you asked for them to stop, or if this is a follow-up to a previous conversation on a certain date/time. Electronic messages, such as email and texts, mark the date and time and may be flagged to provide a "read receipt." If witnesses were present, ask them to document their own detailed account of what happened. Ask for a copy that you keep at home.

Step 3: Report
Depending on the incident, some victims might need to start here, after documenting their experiences as evidence. Report the harassment to a supervisor who is superior to the harasser, and ask that the behaviors be stopped. If the incidents are reported to the supervisor in person, immediately send a follow-up email or memo as documentation.

If there's no change, make a formal complaint with your employer. Keep copies of correspondence sent to, or received from, anyone about the harassment, any reports made, and actions taken.

Sexual harassment is bad for people and business. Your organization has a vested interest in stopping it immediately, so follow due process and allow them to resolve the issue internally.

Get support

Do not keep this to yourself and resist the urge to stay isolated. Remember, sexual harassment is often designed to cause you embarrassment and shame. It's not your fault and you have nothing to hide. There's a good chance it's happened to someone else, and together your stories offer even more powerful evidence. Tell your supervisor, trusted peers, friend, family member, or a counselor. They will offer support and perspective.

Overall, there's safety in numbers. If you're uncomfortable with someone's intentions, do all you can to avoid meeting in private. Conduct business in open settings with other people present.

What to Do if You're a Bystander

"It's none of my business"

Sexual harassment doesn't exist in a bubble. For it to be pervasive or severe, others have to know besides the victim. They're called witnesses, enablers, or bystanders, and that might mean you. While it may be scary to get involved for fear of retaliation, it's absolutely your business. Staying silent makes you complicit.

Why speak up? There are multiple reasons. First, this is your workplace, too; don't you want it to be safe and respectful for all? Sexual harassment is bad for business, that means if left unchecked, it could lead to bad publicity and ultimately hurt you financially. More than that, it can hurt you emotionally. It's very stressful to witness harm and say nothing.

"Someone else will say something, right?"

You might think that the more witnesses there are to sexual harassment, the more people will speak up. The opposite is true. In a well-known study called The Bystander Effect, researchers showed that while most bystanders witnessing someone in distress had empathy, large crowds made them less inclined to offer help.

It's called "diffused responsibility," or the assumption that someone else will handle it. There's also the concern that if no one else is stepping in, maybe it's not really a problem. This is what normalizes bad behavior: Everyone knows yet says nothing.

"What hurts the victim most is not the cruelty of the oppressor, but the silence of the bystander."
— ELIE WIESEL,
Holocaust survivor and Nobel Laureate

But, if one person is brave enough to intervene, others are likely to follow. You could be that positive social influence that turns the tide of support. Don't wait to act assuming someone else is going to step in to help. Assume you're the "someone."

Four ways bystanders can help

1. **If you see something, say something.** Tell the harasser his or her actions are inappropriate. For example, say, "I saw/heard that. It's not right, you need to stop."

2. **Document.** Immediately document what happened. Even if you're unsure if what you observed was sexual harassment, write it down anyway. Note all the specifics such as location, day, time, people involved, what was said or done, what you did, and follow-up conversations. Keep your notes at home. You may never need them, but if something does develop, your notes could be crucial in aiding a victim's case.

3. **Support the victim.** Even if you're unable to say something in the moment, talk to the target later, in private. If you're unsure if what you saw made the person uncomfortable, ask, "Were you OK with it?" Or, validate that what happened was unprofessional and ask how the person is doing. Offer to be a witness for the victim, and accompany your colleague to report the incident.

4. **Become an ally.** Act as a buffer for your co-worker by offering to be present so that he or she never has to be alone with the perpetrator. Or, disrupt a situation by distracting the harasser, changing the subject, or removing the victim from the situation by saying something like, "You're needed in the other room" or "Want to get a cup of coffee?"

What to Do if You're a Perpetrator

Recognizing yourself as a perpetrator is the first step of acknowledging the role you've played in the problem of sexual harassment. Now it's time to play your role in the solution. You can never erase the past, but you can repair some of the damage done and the damage your inaction is currently doing.

This will require forthright honesty about current *and past* behavior, no matter how long ago. It's too easy to minimize past actions as if they don't count. They count for the victim, so they count for you. Complete accountability means there's no going around issues, only through them, to reach a better outcome.

Be aware that making amends will not: 1) automatically make things better for the victim(s) or 2) guarantee forgiveness. These outcomes are the result of choices made by the victim(s), not you. Your purpose is to use the lessons of your mistakes to set an example of how to create a better work environment for all.

5 ways perpetrators can be part of the solution

1. **Acknowledge victims.** Listen to how you've hurt others without minimizing or correcting their stories. Believe them.

2. **Acknowledge your behavior.** Own up to your past and/or current behavior. Admit the truth because it's the right thing to do, not because you got caught or someone is threatening exposure.

3. **Accept the consequences.** There is a cost to keeping secrets and a cost to telling the truth. Unless you are fully accountable, your mistakes cannot be used for good.

4. **Share your story.** You know the mindset and behaviors of a perpetrator. Use your knowledge to educate others and intervene to prevent similar situations.

5. **Get counseling.** Coming to terms with your history may surface strong emotions of guilt, regret, shame, fear, or embarrassment. It's important to manage these feelings in a healthy way.

"There are no words to express my sorrow and regret for the pain I have caused others by words and actions...Repairing the damage will take a lot of time and soul searching and I'm committed to beginning that effort.

It is now my full-time job."

– MATT LAUER, fired anchor, *NBC Today Show*

"Organizational relationships are built on trust and mutual respect."

– MONA SUTPHEN

5.

CREATING A CULTURE OF RESPECT

It Takes an Organization

How do you stop sexual harassment quickly and permanently? Ultimately, it starts with the organizational values. How employees are treated must be as important as products, services, and profits. The good news is, when employees are treated well, the bottom line is positively impacted! So, addressing sexual harassment isn't something on the side, distracting the company from doing business – it's an integral part of a well-run business.

The previous content has focused on behaviors to STOP in order to prevent sexual harassment. It's time to switch gears and focus on what organizations can START doing to create a professional culture.

7 things to start doing

1. **Start with respect.** Crowd out unwanted behaviors by emphasizing positive ones. Start trainings by inviting employees to brainstorm ways to show respectful behavior. How do you treat someone you respect? What's the body language? How do you speak? What's an example of a positive exchange between co-workers?

2. **Establish and communicate a policy.** Think of your policy as a way to communicate corporate culture. Technically, HR is responsible for making sure it's in compliance with state and federal laws, but top leadership needs to be 100% on board. The policy should be easily accessible, either in the employee handbook or online.

Reporting procedures should be clearly outlined as to the roles and responsibilities of all parties involved. Clear guidance and timelines, as well as details on how to access and file claims, should be easily accessible to the employee.

3. **Encourage reporting.** Reward employees for spotting and reporting unwanted behavior. Train supervisors to listen without being dismissive. Create a simple, timely system that allows employees to report behavior in person, through email or even a hotline. Make sure you follow up to let people who reported know that their concerns were seriously addressed. Reporters are not "troublemakers"; they are helping you stay compliant and supporting your organizational goals.

4. **Institute proportional consequences.** There must be clear and firm consequences for sexual harassment, but many researchers suggest that a zero tolerance policy is more hurtful than helpful. If firing is the automatic penalty, some targets may not come forward. Their only goal is to make it stop, not end a career. Some offenses are better corrected through education. With strong reporting, minor offenses can be immediately addressed and corrected. Absolutely have consequences, but make them proportional to the offense.

5. **Offer consistent, effective training.** For training to be effective, it has to be taken seriously and delivered frequently. The message must go beyond the mandatory legal requirements just so employers can check off a box. It has to humanize employees and reinforce at its foundation the organization's culture of respect.

6. Equip bystanders. Teach all employees how to support one another and promote personal accountability in stopping sexual harassment. Emphasize that saying or doing nothing is equivalent to enabling. Provide actual language and examples of ways to speak up, assist targets, and divert harassers. Make it safe to report.

7. Promote more women. Research suggests that companies with more women in management have less sexual harassment. It's partly because harassment flourishes when men are in power and women aren't, and men feel pressure to accept other men's sexualized behavior.

"I'm not concerned with your liking or disliking me...
All I ask is that you respect me as a human being."
— JACKIE ROBINSON,
first black Major League Baseball player

REVIEW &
CLOSING THOUGHTS

Start the Conversation

This handbook has covered a lot of ground. You've learned exactly what sexual harassment is and how it negatively impacts organizational culture by hurting people. You learned what behaviors to stop but also what to start.

The overriding theme is this: A culture of respect leaves no room for sexual harassment. And, a culture of respect is ultimately what's best for the bottom line. Doing the right thing just makes sense.

Now, it's time to start the conversation and keep it going. Talking about topics like sexual harassment makes them less taboo and less likely to occur. Make this topic part of a bigger dialogue that includes organizational goals, workplace culture, productivity, and profits because they are all related.

Next steps

- Share what you've learned with someone else. Learning is more likely to stick when you put concepts in your own words.

- Acknowledge behavior you need to STOP, including staying silent as a bystander.

- Practice behaviors you want to START. Keep in mind how to demonstrate respect and make daily efforts to communicate it to co-workers.

- Continue to stay aware of offensive behaviors. Use the space in the next chapter to note your observations. These examples can be discussed with a supervisor or during group training.

10 Ways Stopping Sexual Harassment Quickly & Permanently Is Good for Business

1. Supports the organization's stated values and principles.

2. Creates a respectable and transparent public reputation for the organization.

3. Creates positive customer perceptions.

4. Adds to a supportive, stable work environment.

5. Makes it easier to recruit, hire, and retain top talent.

6. Reduces stress and conflict.

7. Increases creativity and productivity.

8. Improves employee trust and engagement.

9. Saves money by reducing absences and sick leave.

10. Reduces risk of lawsuits based on inappropriate behavior.

7. ONGOING SEXUAL HARASSMENT BELIEFS AND BEHAVIORS TO STOP

This handbook describes many inappropriate behaviors that are examples of workplace sexual harassment. Is that everything? Absolutely not! Here's your opportunity to continue your learning by describing additional inappropriate beliefs and behaviors that need to STOP.

_____

_____

_____

_____

_____

_____

_____

_____

_____

_____

_____

_____

_____

_____

_____

ABOUT THE AUTHORS

Eric Harvey is founder of walkthetalk.com and a leading expert on positive people practices and high-achieving organizations. He has worked with hundreds of organizations worldwide, including multi-national corporations, leading healthcare providers, high-tech companies, and highly respected nonprofit organizations.

Eric has authored 26 books that have sold millions of copies worldwide, including best-sellers, *Walk the Talk and Get the Results You Want, Walk Awhile in My Shoes* and *Ethics 4 Everyone.*

Eric devotes his time to consulting, writing, and family. He and his wife, Nancy, live in Pensacola Beach, Florida, and are the proud parents of two daughters and have six grandchildren. Learn more by visiting **www.walkthetalk.com**

Susan Fee is a therapist, author, and national speaker based in Seattle, Washington. She delivers training to individuals and corporations on communication skills, conflict resolution, resiliency, and motivation.

She is the author of six other books, including two published by walkthetalk.com, *The Manager's Motivation Handbook* and *How to Develop Positive, Proud, and Productive People.*

Susan developed Circle of F.R.I.E.N.D.S. to teach girls ages 8-14 how to develop healthy relationships, regulate emotions, increase self-esteem, and communicate assertively. She's presented workshops to Girl Scouts, parent groups, schools, and business organizations. Susan believes that every person has a story worth telling and she wants to help young girls in particular tell a powerful one. Learn more by visiting **www.susanfee.com.**

ABOUT THE WALK THE TALK COMPANY

For over 40 years we have been dedicated to one simple goal...one single mission:

to provide you and your organization with high-quality products and services to ensure individual and organizational success.

Walk The Talk resources are designed to:

- Build critical skills and the confidence to apply them
- Develop an organizational culture that attracts and retains the best of the best
- Deal with workplace *tough stuff* like employee performance problems and litigation avoidance
- Create more trust, confidence, and collaboration at all levels
- Help your organization thrive in today's challenging and ever-changing world

How to Order Copies of This Powerful Handbook

Visit walkthetalk.com or call 888.822.9255.

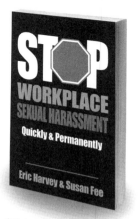

$14.95 per copy
(Quantity discounts available!)

79

WALKTHETALK.COM

Resources for Personal and Professional Success